JURASSIC CLASSICS

the PREHISTORIC MASTERS OF LITERATURE

VOLUME 2

Written by Saskia Lacey • Illustrated by Sernur Isik

WELCOME TO JURASSIC CLASSICS

You're invited to discover the ancient tales dinosaurs once devoured millions of years ago, when the world was a fiercer, but no less literary, place. Jurassic Classics are stories that have been enjoyed by both cold-blooded and warm-blooded readers for eons. They include dinosaur dramas, prehistoric poems, and timeless fossils of fiction. Many of these masterpieces are still studied by scholars today, and they're sure to leave you hungry for more.

The Three Musketeers
THE OLD MAN AND THE SEA
MOBY DICK
THE GREAT GATSBY
The Grapes of Wrath
TO KILL A MOCKINGBIRD
SHERLOCK HOLMES
WAR AND PEACE
TREASURE ISLAND
ADVENTURES OF HUCKLEBERRY FINN
Emma
Hamlet
GREAT EXPECTATIONS

MARK TWAINCERATOPS

The Finest Wit of the Cretaceous Period

The country-bred comic Mark Twainceratops

authored two of the most important works ever written by man or beast.

Born Samuel "Three-Horn" Clemens, the author began using the pen name Mark Twainceratops early in his writing career. The new name gave him the courage to write about topics others feared. Twainceratops had a soft spot for the less fortunate and took a special interest in covering stories of oppressed dinosaurs being trampled by bigger, bolder predators. Adding humor as sharp as an allosaurus' teeth made the serious ideas in Twainceratops' stories more palatable to the common dinosaur.

Mark Twainceratops attempting to surf

THE GOOD OL' DAYS

Mark Twainceratops treasured his childhood years. In those simple times, dinosaurs laughed at the idea of wearing clothes. But as Cretaceous civilization developed, dinosaurs began to see themselves as more than animals. Twainceratops often wrote about the restrictions clothing placed on the simple, beastly nature of dinosaurs. He believed clothes would lead to the eventual downfall of dinosaur civilization.

Like the characters in his literary works, Twainceratops' life was filled with mischief and adventure. The author piloted rafts down the Melted Rock River as a youth. During his travels, he met dinosaurs of all different species, each with a unique story to tell. Some would inspire his most famous characters. Later in life, Twainceratops visited the Patagonian Islands, where he famously witnessed the eruption of the Epicaceous volcano and became the first dinosaur to attempt surfing.

A COLORFUL CHARACTER

At the height of his popularity, Twainceratops was the most famous dinosaur in the world. Instantly recognizable by his white tuft of hair, he could not roam far without encountering a fan. The author relished the attention, stomping across the world and lecturing to large herds. His greatest character was the one he created for himself: the wry and wily humorist, Mark Twainceratops!

With *The Adventures of Tom Sawyer*, Twainceratops wished to remind grown dinosaurs of the fun they had as hatchlings. Tom Sawyer, the novel's main character, is based on the author's fondest memories of childhood. Twainceratops also references many changes that swept the prehistoric world, including hints of the Great Mammal Uprising that was to come. Unfortunately, only fragments of the novel have been uncovered. Archaeologists are hopeful that the full text of this great work will soon be revealed.

The Adventures of Tom Sawyer

BY MARK TWAINCERATOPS

The Adventures of Tom Sawyer

TOM SAWYER
A mischievous hero in no rush to grow up

HUCKLEBERRY FINN
A young rebel who refuses to follow the rules

BECKY THATCHER
Tom's sweetheart and companion

GROWN-UPS
The herd elders who prevent Tom from having fun

A Boring Chore—A Sneaky Idea —Made In the Shade

Saturday morning was come, and there was a happy snarl on every face and a playful stomp in every step. But while others roamed, poor Tom Sawyer was forced to build a fence for his Aunt Polly's cave, bone by bone. It was hard, tail-breaking work.

"Bad luck, old chap! Workin' on a Saturday?" Tom's friend Ben called out.

"Work?" Tom had a sneaky idea. "This ain't work." He turned back to bone sorting, humming cheerfully.

"Come, you don't mean you like it?" Ben looked mighty confused.

"I don't see why not. Does a dinosaur get a chance to build a bone fence every day?"

Ben watched with interest. "Say…Tom, let me build a little."

"No, I reckon it wouldn't do. Aunt Polly's awful particular."

"Oh, shucks, I'll be careful. Lemme try," Ben begged.

Soon Tom was relaxing in the shade, watching Ben and his friends toil over the bone fence. He'd made a great discovery: in order to make a dinosaur want something, it is only necessary to make that thing difficult to attain!

—End of Fragment 122

The Great Escape—A Twinge of Homesickness

Tom had gotten into a full claw fight with his sweetheart, Becky Thatcher. His state of mind was gloomy, and he was convinced t'was only one way to make Miss Becky forgive him—Tom would need to run away.

Now the idea of being by his lonesome did not sit well with young Tom, so he invited his two very best friends, Huckleberry Finn and Joe Harper. Within a day, the friends nested on a small, abandoned island, avoiding all that blame foolishness of life back home. There was much to do, roarin' and stompin' as they pleased, huntin' for turtle eggs, and staying up 'til all hours of the morn. Sitting round the fire, they felt glad-hearted at the glorious freedom they'd found.

But as time passed, an awful mopey feeling came over them. Tom felt it. Huck did too. Joe had been heard crying in his sleep. The plague of homesickness had hit all three islanders. It was time to head back, tail 'tween their legs, and make amends with those they'd left behind.

—End of Fragment 207

An Underground Exploration—Probably, Definitely Lost—The Lava Labyrinth

Becky Thatcher and Tom Sawyer had made up again. It was Becky's birthday, and all of the youngsters were eager to celebrate. The day was to be spent exploring the Midnight Caves, a series of tunnels deep inside a great mountain.

Becky and Tom barreled ahead of their friends, and soon they lost sight of the other explorers.

"Can't you find the way back?" Becky asked. "It's all mixed-up crookedness to me."

"I reckon. But it seems ever so long since we heard the others. I'm getting mighty hungry. We could eat some of those bats—"

Tom was interrupted. A rumble shook through the mountain. Then came the smell that every dinosaur fears, the sulfuric stench of a volcanic eruption.

The two dinosaurs clung to each other and whimpered softly. The great mountain was no mountain. It was a volcano! Molten lava rushed from every direction. Hopping from rock to rock, Becky and Tom dodged the rising lava. How would they ever escape?

—End of Fragment 402

MARK TWAIN

NOVEMBER 30, 1835–APRIL 21, 1910

The Mark Twain archive is much more complete than the Twainceratops fossil record, and the work of this beloved American humorist is frequently studied in schools today. To write his most famous novels, *The Adventures of Tom Sawyer* and *Adventures of Huckleberry Finn*, Twain captured life in the South and drew inspiration from his childhood on the banks of the Mississippi River, which should never be confused with Mark Twainceratops' Melted Rock River.

*"Get your facts first, and . . .
then you can distort 'em as much as you please."*
—Mark Twain, quoted in Rudyard Kipling's From Sea to Sea

Twain was just twelve when his father died. To help, he dropped out of school and found a job as an apprentice at the *Hannibal Courier,* where he was paid with rations of food. When he was 15, he left to work at the *Hannibal Western Union*, a newspaper owned by his brother, Orion. Journalism was a natural fit, but in 1857, Twain landed his dream job—working as a steamboat pilot on the Mississippi River, until the outbreak of the Civil War forced him to return to life on land.

Twain found work as a reporter for the *Virginia City Territorial Enterprise*. There, he wrote stories, editorials, and sketches. Born Samuel Langhorne Clemens, he adopted his pen name, Mark Twain, which is slang for "12 feet of water," and reminiscent of Twain's time on his beloved steamboats. He developed a persona to match his new name—one that was funny, satirical, and approachable. Twain's big break came when his story "Jim Smiley and His Jumping Frog" appeared in publications around the country. Two years later, when his novel—*The Innocents Abroad*—became a bestseller, Twain became one of the most famous writers in America.

Though prejudice still remains a painful issue in modern times, books like Twain's *Adventures of Huckleberry Finn* have changed the way people see each other and have encouraged equality. The book was published when many people were horribly mistreated based on the color of their skin. Huck's travels down the Mississippi River with Jim, a runaway slave, opened readers' eyes to the injustices and prejudices slaves endured.

POPULAR WORKS

The Adventures of Tom Sawyer
Adventures of Huckleberry Finn
The Prince and the Pauper
A Connecticut Yankee in King Arthur's Court
The Tragedy of Pudd'nhead Wilson
The Diary of Adam and Eve
Life on the Mississippi

CHARLES DICKENSODOCUS

Defender of the Downtrodden

Wildly popular with large herds of dinosaurs,

Charles Dickensodocus wrote some of the greatest masterpieces of prehistoric literature, including *Oliver Twist* and *A Christmas Carol.*

As a young dinosaur, Dickensodocus struggled with poverty and hunger. As a result, he was forced to stomp long hours at a berry factory, working hard but earning little. When the author learned the berry juice was used to dye the frills of aristocrats, he roared at the injustice of being a lowborn dinosaur.

Although small-skulled diplodocuses were not known for their cunning minds, Dickensodocus went on to use his experiences toiling for the privileged as fuel for his novels. In his nonfiction works, the author championed the rights of poor and powerless dinosaurs, earning him the title, Defender of the Downtrodden.

Poor Charles working in a berry factory as a boy

A HERD OF HIS OWN

Charles Dickensodocus and his wife, Catherine, had a bountiful brood. The author named each of his offspring after his favorite authors and gave them strange nicknames, including Young Skull and Chicken Stalker. Dickensodocus and his wife had 10 hatchlings in all.

GAD'S HILL PLACE

When Dickensodocus was a half-starved hatchling, he and his father visited Gad's Hill Place. A plant-eater's paradise, the grand manor boasted endless groves of tasty greenery. Dickensodocus vowed to rise through the herds and prove that he was worthy of the leafy haven. Many years later, after Charles had written *A Tale of Two Cities*, he purchased the property and made Gad's Hill Place his domain.

Although Dickensodocus lived long after the Plant-Eater Revolution, he deeply understood the fury of the oppressed. As a former factory worker, he sympathized with the lowborn herds who were forced to labor long hours in beastly conditions. Dickensodocus favored change, but he did not support violent revolution. Some of the most memorable—and terrifying—moments in *A Tale of Two Cities* describe wild-eyed revolutionaries blindly trampling the aristocratic herds. With his dark descriptions of the mad stampedes, the author made his preference for peace clear, and his vision continues to echo across the millennia today.

A Tale of Two Cities

BY CHARLES DICKENSODOCUS

A Tale of Two Cities

SYDNEY CARTON
The depressed dinosaur who is forever changed by his love for Lucie Manette

LUCIE MANETTE
The pure-hearted and prim fiancée of Charles Darnay

CHARLES DARNAY
The honorable aristocrat who rejects the privileges of his cruel and wealthy family

THE PLANT-EATER REVOLUTION
The gruesome war between the aristocracy and the mistreated herbivores

It was the best of times. It was the worst of times. Dinosaurs reigned supreme over the prehistoric kingdom, but within their reptilian ranks there was great animosity. For the differences between the carnivores and herbivores were so monstrous that it was as if they lived in two different cities.

In those bleak days, the carnivorous dinosaurs formed a terrible aristocracy. They used herbivores for their every wish and whim, forcing them to work long hours in poor conditions. The plant-eaters, who were naturally peaceful dinosaurs, grew restless under the brutal rule of the carnivores. Their grumbles and growls soon turned to roars, and the mad stampedes began. Herds of plant-eaters raged through the homes of the aristocracy, capturing every carnivore they could get their claws on.

But even in terrible times, love shined in the darkest of hearts. Such was the case of Sydney Carton, a hard-hearted dinosaur who cared little about his own well being, much less the outcome of the Plant-Eater Revolution.

Sydney's indifferent attitude was suddenly changed at the trial of Charles Darnay, an aristocratic dinosaur whom many herbivores would love if it were not for his carnivorous ancestry. For that, the herd would never forgive him.

Looking over the Valley of Justice, Sydney grumbled, "Why do I even bother to watch these dull theatrics? Nothing in this pointless life matters!" The dinosaur was about to take a nap when he saw the gentle snout of Lucie Manette.

"Who is that lovely dinosaur on the witness mound?" he gazed, mouth agape. Lucie's scales seemed to glow. Sydney was mesmerized.

"Yes." Lucie nodded sadly. "It was dark, but I am sure it was him…" She stared sorrowfully at Charles Darnay, knowing her testimony would lead to his imprisonment. Sydney was moved by Lucie's pity for the captured beast. Through the trees, the roars of the Plant-Eater Revolution grew louder. It was time for Sydney to take a side in this war, for Lucie's sake and that of his herd.

Sydney inspected Charles Darnay, taking in every detail of the reptile. He had an idea, though he wasn't sure it would work. Sydney lumbered forward and hissed an idea in the ear of Darnay's lawyer.

The lawyer spoke, "Your honor, it seems we have a new line of defense. Would you not agree that my colleague looks much like Charles Darnay?"

The judge squinted at Sydney and then looked back at Darnay. "Why, yes. Their appearance is quite similar."

"Is it not then possible that the prosecution may have mistook Darnay for another dinosaur?

"It is possible." The judge nodded solemnly.

"What madness is this?" the herds howled, hungry for justice.

But hours later, Darnay was allowed to roam free. Sydney looked on as Lucie smiled, happy to see her happy—though he knew Lucie was in love with Darnay.

Lucie and Darnay never forgot Sydney's noble nature and named their first child Sydney Jr. The gruesome Plant-Eater Revolution still loomed, but the Darnays found comfort in their small family—and Sydney in Lucie's happiness.

CHARLES DICKENS

FEBRUARY 7, 1812–JUNE 9, 1870

FROM BIRTH UNTIL OLD AGE, THE ENGLISH NOVELIST CHARLES DICKENS was never confused with a diplodocus, but sadly, the tragedies he wrote about were even more desperate than the Plant-Eater Revolution. Born in 1812, Dickens lived in tumultuous times, and like many novelists, his work reflects the war and poverty that were all too real in his lifetime.

"Reflect upon your present blessings—of which every man has many—not on your past misfortunes, of which all men have some."
—A Christmas Carol

At twelve years old, Dickens was forced to leave school and work at a boot-blacking factory. He earned a mere six shillings a week and was happy when, at fifteen, he got a job as a clerk in a solicitor's office. Soon after, he began freelancing as a court reporter and eventually became a writer. In 1833, Dickens began submitting sketches to several publications under the pen name "Boz." The success of his first book, *Sketches by Boz*, caught the attention of Catherine Hogarth, who would one day become his wife and the mother of his ten children. As his work grew in popularity, Dickens celebrated by moving into Gad's Hill Place, a mansion he had once admired during more desperate days.

Dickens achieved wider popularity during his lifetime than any author who came before him, and he is considered the greatest writer of England's Victorian era. Later in life, he could not leave home for a stroll through the city without being recognized. Part of this popularity was due to the way he published his novels. From November to April 1859, *A Tale of Two Cities* was published in weekly installments in *All the Year Round*, a magazine founded by the author. This serial format left audiences breathless for more and forced Dickens to write quickly. The prolific author wrote 16 novels during his career, including classics such as *Oliver Twist*, *A Christmas Carol*, and *Great Expectations*.

POPULAR WORKS

Great Expectations
A Tale of Two Cities
David Copperfield
Oliver Twist
Nicholas Nickleby
The Pickwick Papers
A Christmas Carol

JANE AUSTENLOVENATOR

Clever Critic of High Reptilian Society

Let us finish with a fierce tribute
to the master of manners, Jane Austenlovenator.

Unlike other dinosaur authors, who roared for recognition, Austenlovenator wrote in secret, hiding her work from everyone but her family. Much of her work was written as her mother and sister daintily picked through a pile of bones, in the cramped cave that served as the Austenlovenators' sitting room. Despite a lack of privacy, Jane was wildly productive, writing six novels over the course of her short life.

Everyone in the Austenlovenator herd was supportive of Jane's writing. Herd members hunted for her, and unlike other dinosauresses, Jane spent little time sharpening her claws, which allowed her time to write and revise. In the evenings, Jane read her work aloud to the family.

Jane Austenlovenator reading aloud to her family

While many prehistoric writers might find life in a small, quiet territory limiting, Jane used it to her advantage. Later in life, she declared the lives of "three or four herds in a country village as the perfect subject for a novel."

AN ELEGANT MUD BATH

Austenlovenator spent most of her life enjoying the quiet countryside. However, she did spend several years in Mud Bath, a town where dinosaurs from many different territories gathered to frolic in its famous mud pools. While at Mud Bath, she got a close look at the habits and attitudes of the upper class—knowledge she would put to great use in her novels!

In *Pride and Prejudice*, Mr. Darcy is a well-bred predator with a refined sense of smell, and his large territory places him in the upper ranks of prehistoric society. He could easily have his pick of mates, and in those days, to refuse such a dinosaur's claw in marriage would have been unthinkable.

But like Austenlovenator, the heroine Elizabeth Bennet stomps to her own beat. Elizabeth is well aware that with a mate like Mr. Darcy she would never go hungry, but she still denies Mr. Darcy's proposal, an act that was as ferociously independent as a lady dinosaur writing books. Austenlovenator's literary courage continues to inspire writers of all species millions of years later.

THE RULES OF SOCIETY

Unlike so many of Austenlovenator's fictional characters, the author herself never married. In her late twenties, she refused a marriage proposal from a well-bred dinosaur. Scholars debate if Austenlovenator turned down the proposal because she knew being a wife and mother would restrict her freedom to write and roam.

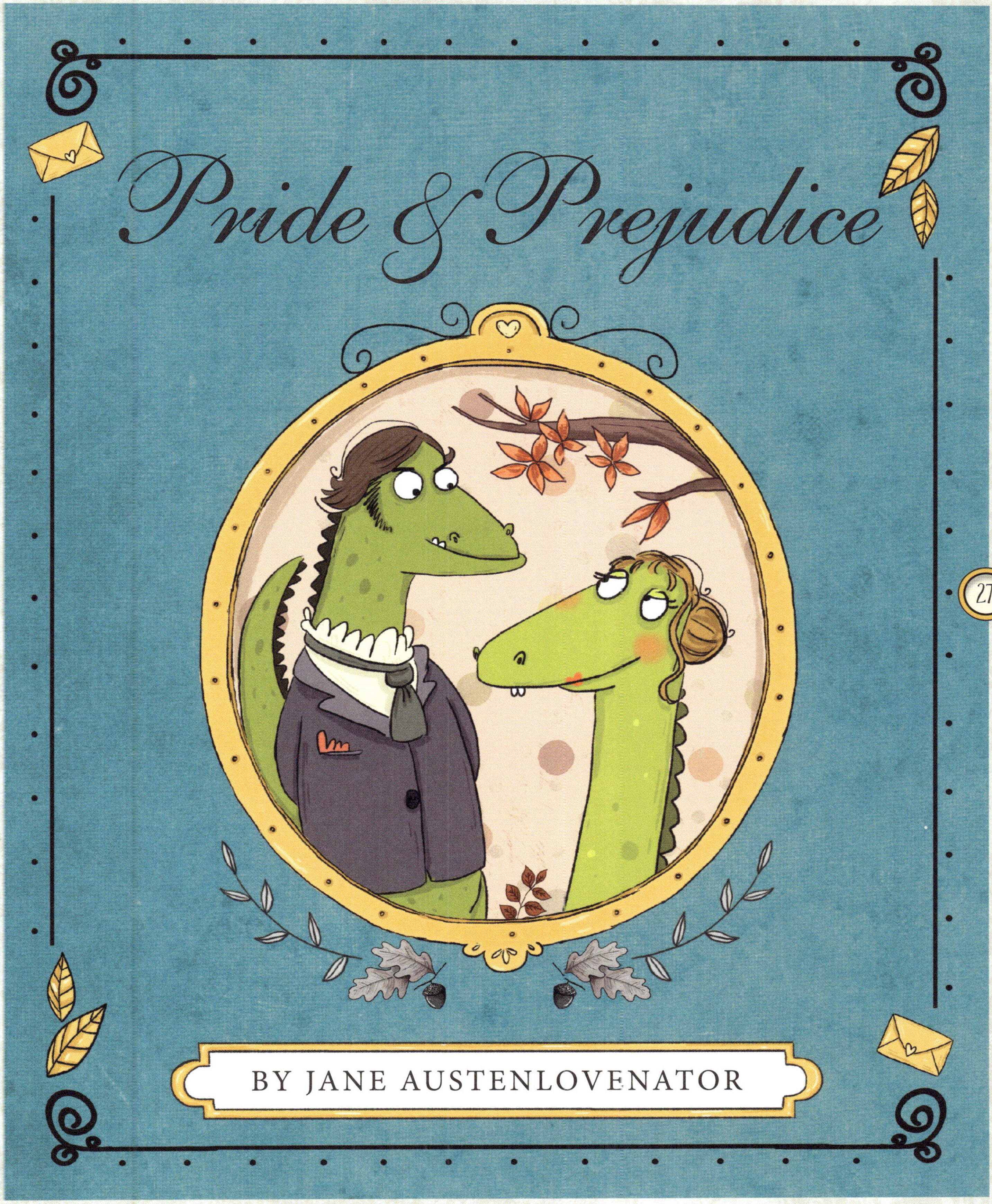
Pride & Prejudice
BY JANE AUSTENLOVENATOR

Pride & Prejudice

ELIZABETH BENNET

A lively lady who refuses to follow the rules of dinosaur courtship

MR. DARCY

An exceedingly proud gentleman with a large territory

It is a truth universally acknowledged, that a dinosaur in possession of a large territory shall attract many mates. But Elizabeth Bennet, a spirited and clever dinosauress, valued love above wealth and property. She hoped to find her true mate at an upcoming dance, the Beastly Ball.

A newcomer of fine breeding, Mr. Darcy, was also in attendance. With handsome tail and noble gait, the gentleman was known to own vast lands. He was not, however, fond of dancing.

"I detest hopping about like a fool," scoffed Mr. Darcy. "There is not a lady reptile here whom it would not be a punishment for me to stomp with."

"What about the fine-feathered dinosauress behind you?" an aristocratic pterodactyl asked.

Darcy sniffed in Elizabeth's direction. "She is tolerable, but not sweet-scented enough to tempt me."

Elizabeth snarled in fury. Why had she thought she would fall in love at the Beastly Ball? Mr. Darcy was surely the most disagreeable dinosaur to ever exist!

A gust of wind carried Elizabeth's scent to Darcy's flared nostrils as she walked away. Hers was the playful perfume of an independent spirit. The Jurassic gentleman immediately fell snout over tail in love.

That spring, Elizabeth made Mr. Darcy's acquaintance surprisingly often. She saw him at the watering hole, out hunting, and more than a few times as she scampered through the countryside.

Spying Mr. Darcy from afar, she tried to hurry away, but Darcy saw Elizabeth and charged in her direction. "My fierce feelings will not be tamed. You must allow me to howl my love from the highest treetops."

Elizabeth tilted her head in confusion. "Your feelings?" She was astonished, but

unmoved. "I never desired your wild affection."

"This is all the reply which I am to have the honor of expecting?" Darcy asked desperately.

"Nothing would tempt me to accept a dinosaur who would be so cold-blooded as to speak poorly of my scent." Elizabeth swiped at Darcy, growling angrily. Then, turning her back to him, she stomped home.

Darcy roamed the valley, miserable, but too proud to return. Gossips whispered that he refused to sniff lady reptiles who were only interested in riches and nothing more. Elizabeth wondered if she had misjudged Darcy.

When she next saw him at her family's estate, she found herself nervous. Her heart fluttered, and she was only able to retain her silence for a few moments before saying, "Mr. Darcy, I am a selfish beast and can no longer help wishing we could start again."

Darcy pawed the ground. He took a deep breath and gathered his courage. "If your feelings are unchanged, tell me so at once. My fierce affection for you is as untamed as ever."

"Dear, Darcy, my heart is transformed."

Encouraged, Darcy quickly offered his claw in marriage. Elizabeth roared joyfully and accepted. Each promised the other that neither pride nor prejudice would divide their love again.

JANE AUSTEN

December 16, 1775–July 18, 1817

Jane Austen's claws were not as sharp as those found on her reptilian kin, but her mind was just as keen. Still adored centuries after her books were first published, Austen is celebrated for her wry observations on high society and the human heart.

"The person, be it gentleman or lady, who has not pleasure in a good novel, must be intolerably stupid."
—Northanger Abbey

As a child, Austen spent hours reading in her father's vast library, playing games with her seven siblings, and putting on plays for her family. As she grew older, Austen began writing novels, short stories, poems, and plays. Her work was witty and focused on romantic relationships—characteristics she'd become known for.

Much of Austen's early life was spent helping run the family home, attending church, playing piano, and socializing with neighbors. Some nights, Austen would choose a novel to read aloud to the family. Occasionally, she would even read something she had written herself. Though she was constantly writing, she didn't attempt to publish her work until later in life. She began drafts of *Elinor and Marianne*, which would later be published as *Sense and Sensibility*, and *First Impressions*, which would later be published as *Pride and Prejudice*. Both of these novels would become two of Austen's most celebrated works, focusing on ordinary people engaged in the trials and triumphs of everyday life.

Although her novels were often about marriage, Austen herself never married; instead, she developed her craft. From 1811 to 1817, six of Austen's novels were published anonymously, each widely read and enjoyed—so much in fact that the prince regent discreetly commanded that *Emma* be dedicated to him.

It was only upon Austen's death that her literary talent was recognized. Today, her work is famous, and she remains one of the most beloved authors of all time.

POPULAR WORKS

Sense and Sensibility
Pride and Prejudice
Emma
Persuasion

This library edition published in 2018 by Walter Foster Jr.,
an imprint of The Quarto Group
6 Orchard Road, Suite 100
Lake Forest, CA 92630

Written by Saskia Lacey
Edited by Heidi Fiedler
Illustrated by Sernur Isik

Distributed in the United States and Canada by
Lerner Publisher Services
241 First Avenue North
Minneapolis, MN 55401 U.S.A.
www.lernerbooks.com

First Library Edition

Library of Congress Cataloging-in-Publication Data

Names: Lacey, Saskia, author. | Isik, Sernur, illustrator.
Title: The prehistoric masters of literature / written by Saskia Lacey ; illustrated by Sernur Isik.
Description: Lake Forest, CA : Quarto Group, [2017] | Series: Jurassic classics | Summary: "Famous literary figures are given dinosaur-inspired pseudonyms and prehistoric biographies as a way of introducing young readers to classic literature"-- Provided by publisher. Contents: Volume 1: William Shakespeareasaurus -- The Brontesaurus sisters -- Edgar Allan Terrordactyl. Contents: Volume 2: Mark Twainceratops -- Charles Dickensodocus -- Jane Austenlovenator.
Identifiers: LCCN 2017035002| ISBN 9781942875550 (v. 1 : hardcover) | ISBN 9781942875567 (v. 2 : hardcover)
Subjects: LCSH: Canon (Literature)--Parodies, imitations, etc.--Juvenile literature. | Authors--Biography--Juvenile literature. | Shakespeare, William, 1564-1616--Juvenile literature. | Brontë, Anne, 1820-1849--Juvenile literature. | Brontë, Charlotte, 1816-1855--Juvenile literature. | Brontë, Emily, 1818-1848--Juvenile literature. | Poe, Edgar Allan, 1809-1849--Juvenile literature. | Twain, Mark, 1835-1910--Juvenile literature. | Dickens, Charles, 1812-1870--Juvenile literature. | Austen, Jane, 1775-1817--Juvenile literature. | CYAC: Humorous stories. | Dinosaurs--Fiction. | Authors--Fiction.
Classification: LCC PZ7.1.L2 Pr 2017 | DDC [Fic]--dc23
LC record available at https://lccn.loc.gov/2017035002

Printed in USA
9 8 7 6 5 4 3 2 1

MIX
Paper from responsible sources
FSC® C008080